C000240764

COUNTED THREAD EMBROIDERY

Edith Hansen & Ingrid Hansen

VAN NOSTRAND REINHOLD COMPANY

New York   Cincinnati   Toronto   London   Melbourne

Van Nostrand Reinhold Company Regional Offices
New York Cincinnati Chicago Millbrae Dallas

Van Nostrand Reinhold Company International
Offices
Toronto Melbourne London

This book was originally published by Høst &
Søns, Copenhagen, Denmark

Copyright © 1968, Selskabet til Haandarbejdets
Fremme, Copenhagen

Library of Congress Catalog Card No. 73 15284
ISBN 0 442 30024 7

All rights reserved. No part of this work covered
by the copyright hereon may be reproduced or
used in any form or by any means – graphic,
electronic, or mechanical, including
photocopying, recording, taping or information
storage and retrieval systems – without written
permission of the publisher.

This book is printed in Great Britain by Jolly and
Barber Ltd., Rugby and bound by the Ferndale
Book Company.
Photography by Bent Hassing
Published by Van Nostrand Reinhold Company,
Inc., 450 West 33rd St., New York, N.Y. 10001
and Van Nostrand Reinhold Company Ltd.,
Egginton House, 25-28 Buckingham Gate,
London S.W.1.

16 15 14 13 12 11 10 9 8 7 6 5 4 3 2 1

It has long been the wish of the Danish Handcraft Guild to publish a book of counted thread embroidery patterns. The technique has always been taught in Danish schools, even to quite young children. It is simple and pleasant to do and soon produces satisfying results.

The two authors have produced many new patterns, although some of these have been inspired by traditional patterns. Both materials and designs have been adapted to suit modern requirements. To obtain the best results it is advisable to use the recommended thread and fabrics; the effectiveness of a simple technique such as this often depends on the correct choice of materials.

We hope that the book will be widely used, since all the patterns can be adapted to many different uses in interior decoration.

Gertie Wandel
President of the Danish Handcraft Guild.

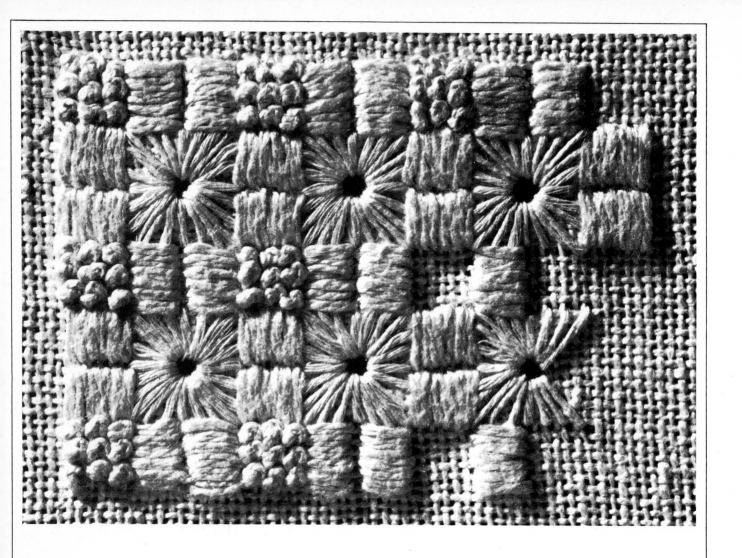

Cushion
Geometric Satin Stitch, Eye Stitch and French Knots

Unbleached Hanne linen 63" (160 cm) wide. Overall measurement $15\frac{3}{4}" \times 27\frac{1}{2}"$ (40 × 70 cm). Finished work about $11\frac{3}{4}" \times 11\frac{3}{4}"$ (30 × 30 cm). Linen thread quality E and K. Eye stitch worked with quality E, whole thickness. French knots and satin stitches with quality K, 2 strands. At upper left-hand corner of linen measure 2" (5 cm) in from side edge and down from top edge. Start at this point. The two sides of the cushion are made in one piece. The seam is stitched close up to the embroidery.

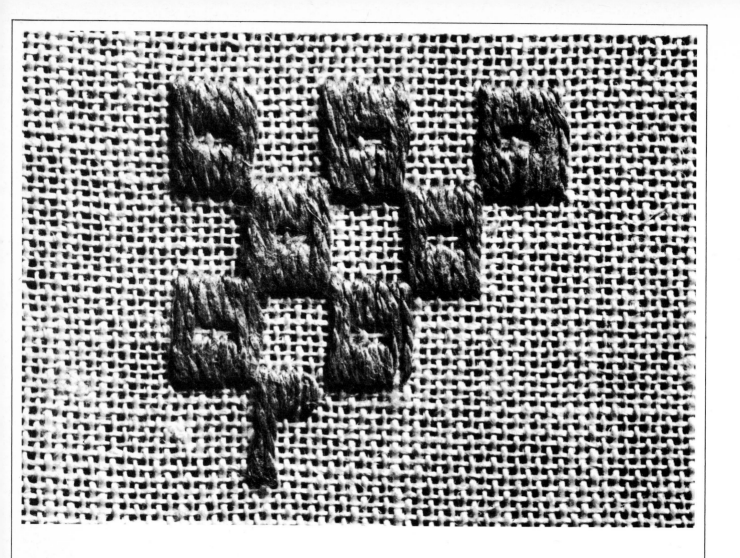

Cushion

Geometric Satin Stitch

Bleached or unbleached D linen 55″ (140 cm) wide. Overall measurement $16\frac{1}{2}″ \times 26\frac{3}{4}″$ (42×68 cm). Finished work about $11\frac{1}{2}″ \times 12\frac{1}{2}″$ (29×31 cm). Linen thread quality K. Work with 1 strand. At upper left-hand corner of linen measure 2″ (5 cm) in from side edge and down from top edge. Start at this point. The two sides of the cushion are made in one piece. The seams are stitched close up to the embroidery.

Cushion

Geometric Satin Stitch and Long-Armed Cross Stitch

Bleached Hanne linen 63″ (160 cm) wide. Overall measurement $18\frac{1}{8}″$ × $23\frac{3}{4}″$ (46 × 60 cm). Finished work $10\frac{1}{4}″$ × $14\frac{1}{4}″$ (26 × 36 cm). Linen thread quality E. Work with whole thickness. At upper left-hand corner of linen measure 2″ (5 cm) in from side edge and down from top edge. Start at this point. The two sides of the cushion are made in one piece. Make up the cushion with the seams close up to the embroidery.

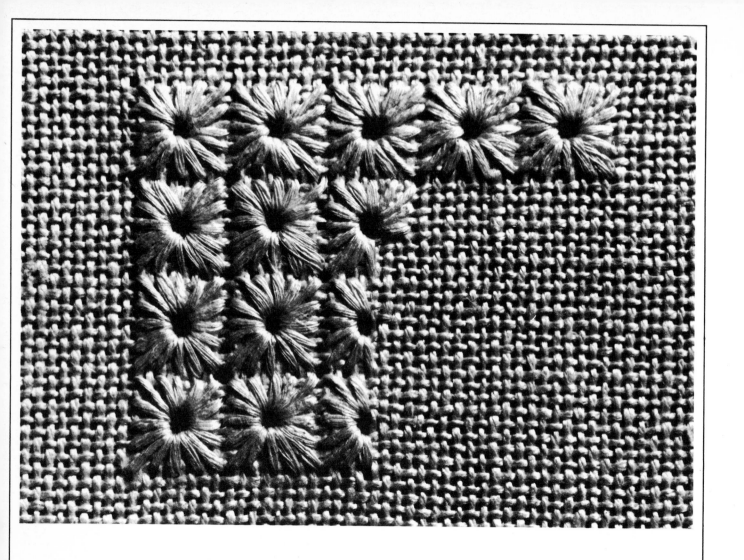

Placemat
Eyestitch

Bleached Hanne linen 63″ (160 cm) wide. Overall measurement 20″ × 16⅜″ (51 × 41·5 cm). Finished work about 16⅛″ × 12⅜″ (41 × 31·5 cm). Linen thread quality E. Work with 1 strand. At upper left-hand corner of linen measure 2″ (5 cm) in from side edge and down from top edge. Start at this point. Hem: fold the material 1 thread from embroidery all the way round. Hem is 8 threads wide.

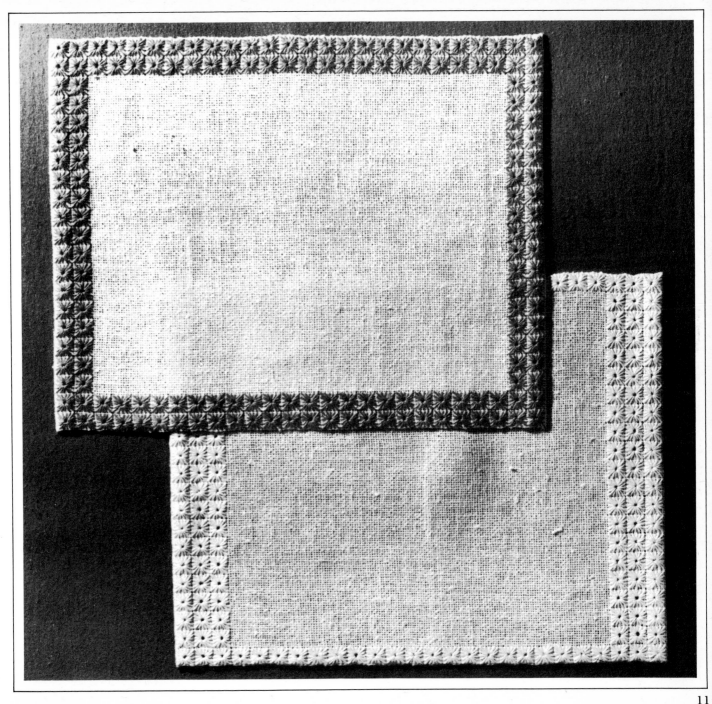

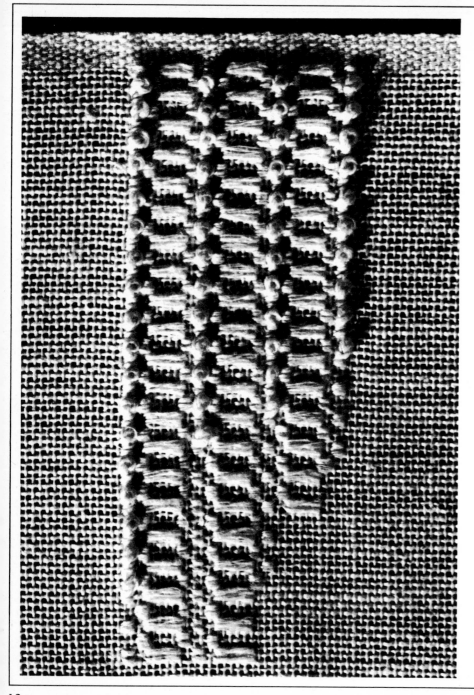

Placemat

Geometric Satin Stitch and French Knots

Bleached D linen $11\frac{3}{4}''$ (30 cm) wide. Overall measurement $11\frac{3}{4}'' \times 19''$ (30 $\times$ 48 cm). Finished work $11\frac{3}{4}'' \times 16\frac{3}{4}''$ (30 $\times$ 40 cm). Linen thread quality E. Satin stitch is worked with half a strand, French knots with 2 strands. At upper left-hand corner of linen measure $1\frac{3}{4}''$ (4 cm) in from side edge. Start working 1 thread from selvedge. Hem: fold the material 1 thread from embroidery. Hem is 6 threads wide.

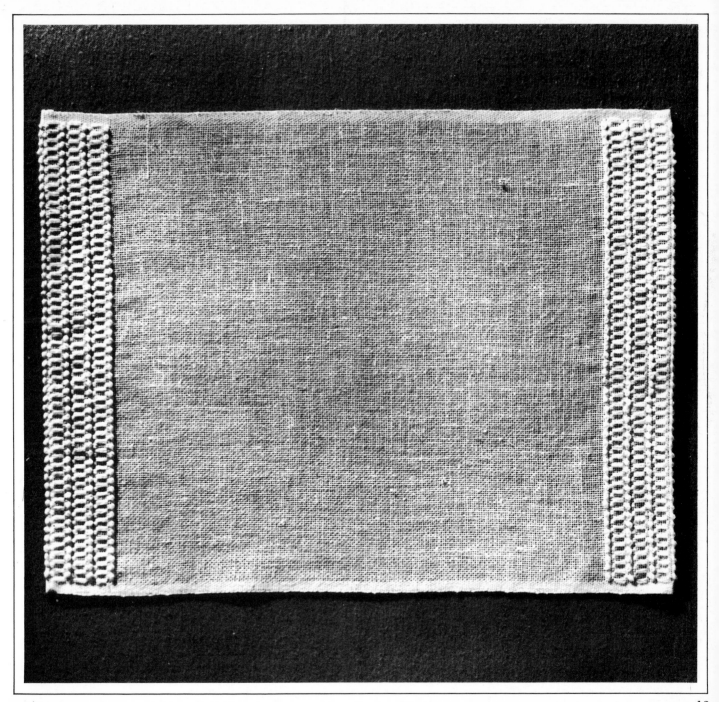

Placemat

Eye Stitch, Geometric Satin Stitch and French Knots

Bleached Hanne linen 13″ (33 cm) wide. Overall measurement 13″ × 19¾″ (33 × 50 cm). Finished work about 13″ × 16⅛″ (33 × 41 cm). Linen thread quality E and K. Eye stitch is worked with quality E, whole thickness; satin stitches and French knots with quality K, 2 strands. At upper left-hand corner of linen measure 1¾″ (4·5 cm) in from side edge and count 1 thread down. Start at this point. Hem: fold the material 2 threads from embroidery. Hem is 6 threads wide.

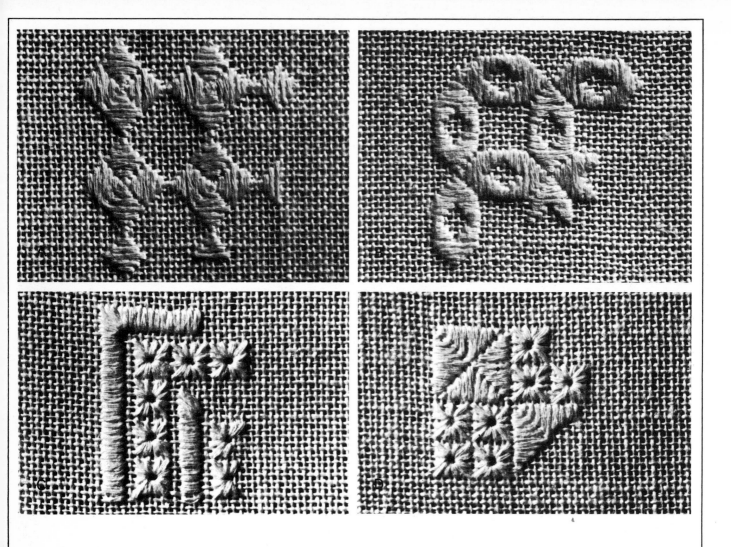

Small Mats

Geometric Satin Stitch and Eye Stitch

Bleached D linen 55″ (140 cm) wide. Overall measurement $7\frac{7}{8}″ \times 7\frac{7}{8}″$ (20 $\times$ 20 cm). Finished work about $5\frac{1}{2}″ \times 5\frac{1}{2}″$ (14 $\times$ 14 cm). Linen thread quality E. Work with half a strand. Find the middle of the material and start at this point. For A, fold the material 3 threads from embroidery; for B and C, 4 threads from embroidery; and for D, 6 threads from embroidery. Hem is 6 threads wide.

16

Placemat

Geometric Satin Stitch and French Knots

Bleached D linen $11\frac{3}{4}''$ (30 cm) wide. Overall measurement $11\frac{3}{4}'' \times 19\frac{3}{4}''$ (30 × 50 cm). Finished work about $11\frac{3}{4}'' \times 16\frac{1}{4}''$ (30 × 41·5 cm). Linen thread quality E. Satin stitch: work with half a strand. French knots: work with 2 strands. At upper left-hand corner of linen measure 2″ (5 cm) in from side edge. Start to work 1 thread away from the selvedge. Hem: fold the material 6 threads from embroidery at the ends. Hem is 6 threads wide.

19

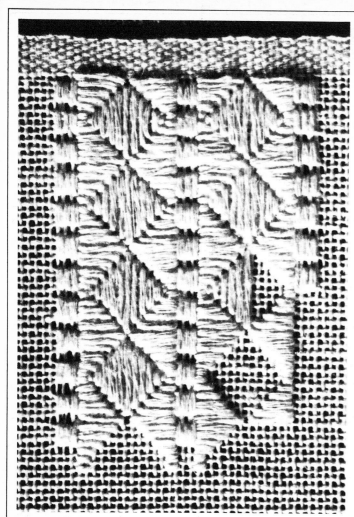
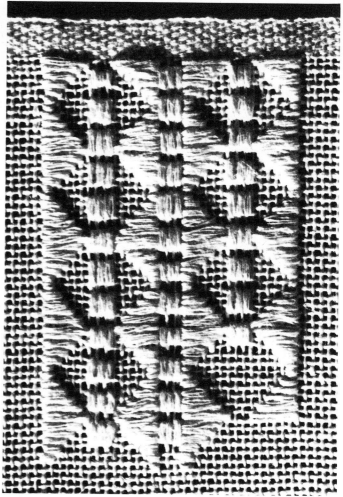

Placemat

Geometric Satin Stitch

Bleached D linen $11\frac{3}{4}''$ (30 cm) wide. Overall measurement $11\frac{3}{4}'' \times 19\frac{1}{4}''$ (30 × 49 cm). Finished work $11\frac{3}{4}'' \times 16\frac{1}{8}''$ (30 × 41 cm). Linen thread quality E. Work with half a strand. At upper left-hand corner measure 2″ (5 cm) in, and start embroidery 1 thread away from selvedge. Hem: fold the material 6 threads from embroidery. Hem is 6 threads wide.

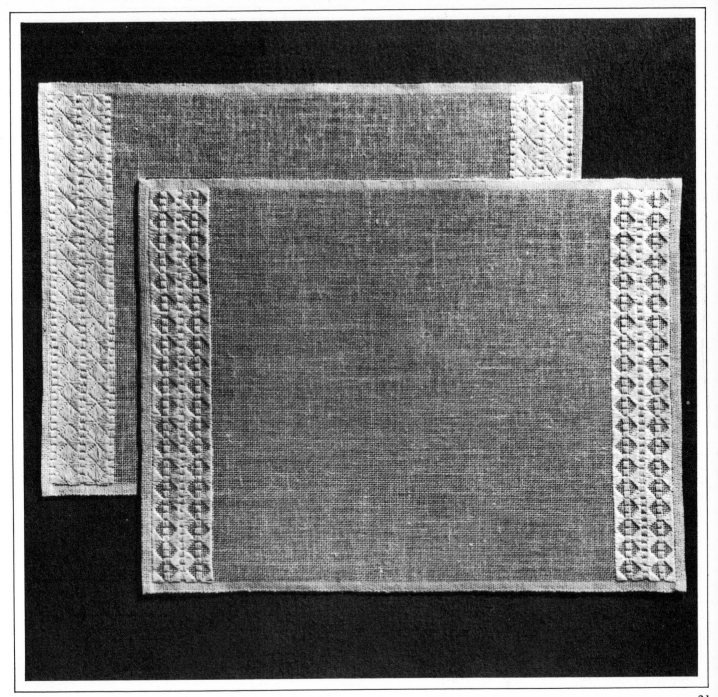

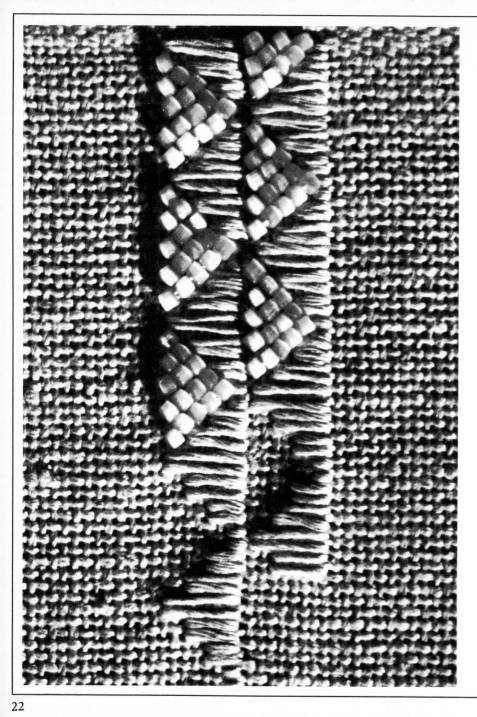

Placemat

Geometric Satin Stitch and Beads

Bleached Hanne linen 13″ (33 cm) wide. White beads. Overall measurement 13″ × 19¾″ (33 × 50 cm). Finished work about 13″ × 16½″ (33 × 42 cm). Linen thread quality E. Work with whole thickness. At upper left-hand corner of linen measure 1¾″ (4·5 cm) in from side edge and count 5 threads down from outer edge. Start at this point. The satin stitches are worked first. The beads are stitched on with 2 strands of stranded cotton. Hem: fold the material 2 threads from embroidery. Hem is 6 threads wide.

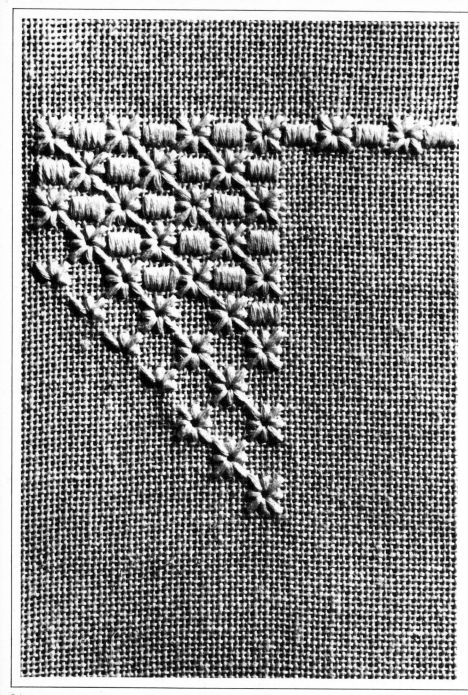

Placemat

Geometric Satin Stitch and Eye Stitch

Bleached D linen 55″ (140 cm) wide. Overall measurement $15\frac{1}{8}″ \times 19″$ (38·5 × 48 cm). Finished work about $12″ \times 15\frac{3}{4}″$ (30·5 × 40 cm). Linen thread quality E. Work with whole thickness. At upper left-hand corner of linen measure $1\frac{3}{4}″$ (4 cm) from side edge and down from top edge. Start to work at this point. Hem: fold the material 2 threads from embroidery all the way round. Hem is 8 threads wide.

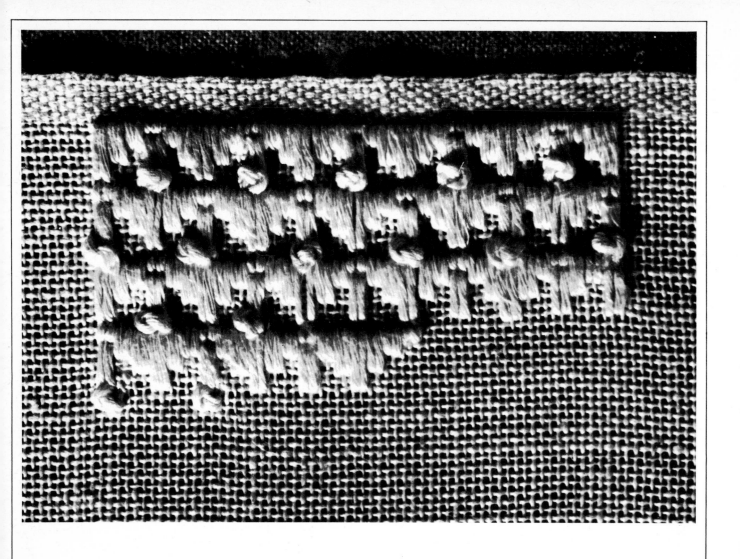

Placemat

Geometric Satin Stitch and French Knots

Bleached D linen $11\frac{3}{4}''$ (30 cm) wide. Overall measurement $11\frac{3}{4}'' \times 19\frac{1}{4}''$ (30 × 49 cm). Finished work about $11\frac{3}{4}'' \times 16\frac{1}{8}''$ (30 × 41 cm). Linen thread quality E. Satin stitch: work with whole thickness. French knots: work with 2 strands. At upper left-hand corner measure 2″ (5 cm) in and start to work exactly where selvedge starts. Hem: fold the material 7 threads from embroidery. Finish with a hemstitch over 2 threads. Hem is 6 threads wide.

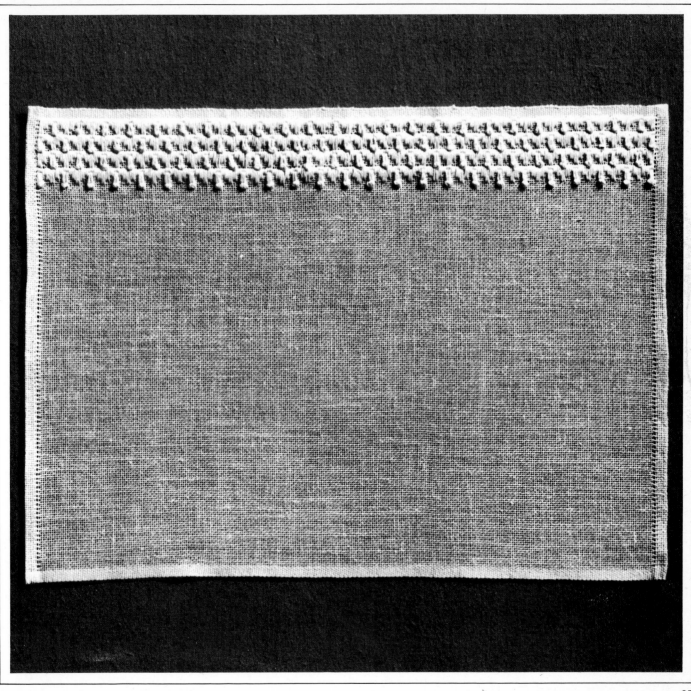

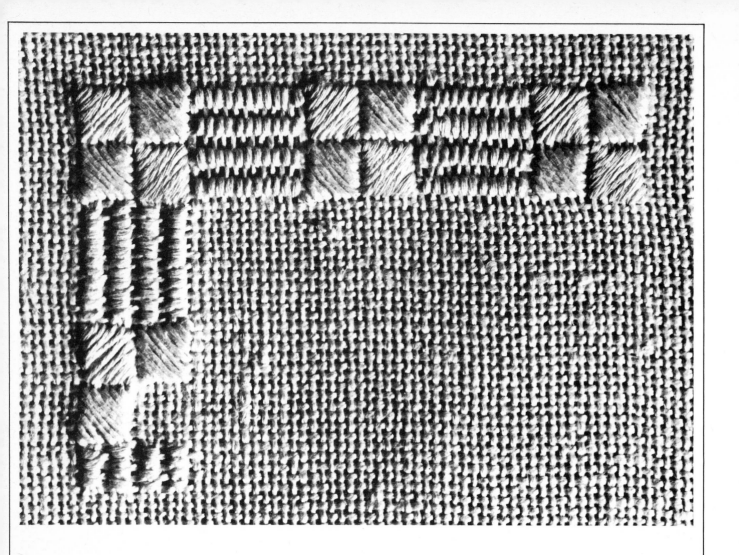

Square Placemat
Geometric Satin Stitch

Bleached Hanne linen 63″ (160 cm) wide. Overall measurement 14½″ × 14½″ (37 × 37 cm). Finished work 11½″ × 11½″ (29 × 29 cm). Linen thread quality E. Work with whole thickness. At upper left-hand corner of linen measure 1½″ (4 cm) from side edge and down from top edge. Start at this point. Hem: fold the material right to the border. Hem is 6 threads wide.

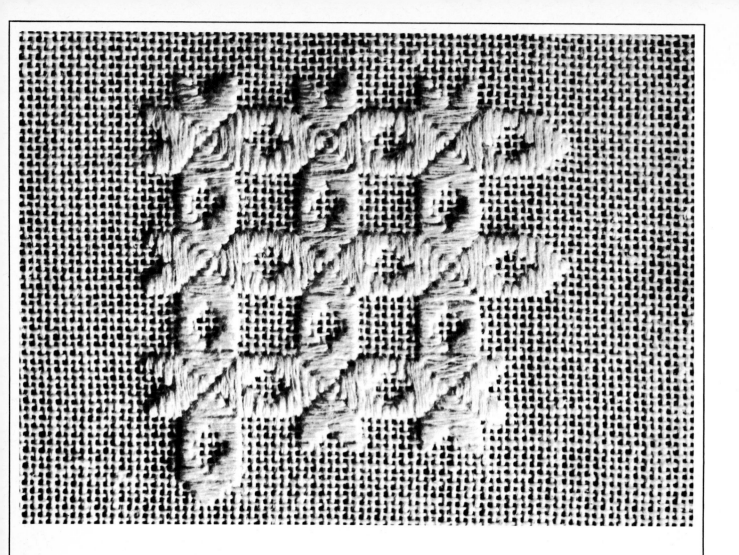

Square Placemat
Geometric Satin Stitch

Bleached D linen 55″ (140 cm) wide. Overall measurement $15\frac{3}{4}″ \times 15\frac{3}{4}″$ (40 × 40 cm). Finished work $12\frac{1}{2}″ \times 12\frac{1}{2}″$ (32 × 32 cm). Linen thread quality E. Work with whole thickness. At upper left-hand corner of linen measure $1\frac{1}{2}″$ (4 cm) in from side edge and down from top edge. Start at this point. Hem: fold the material 2 threads from embroidery. Hem is 8 threads wide.

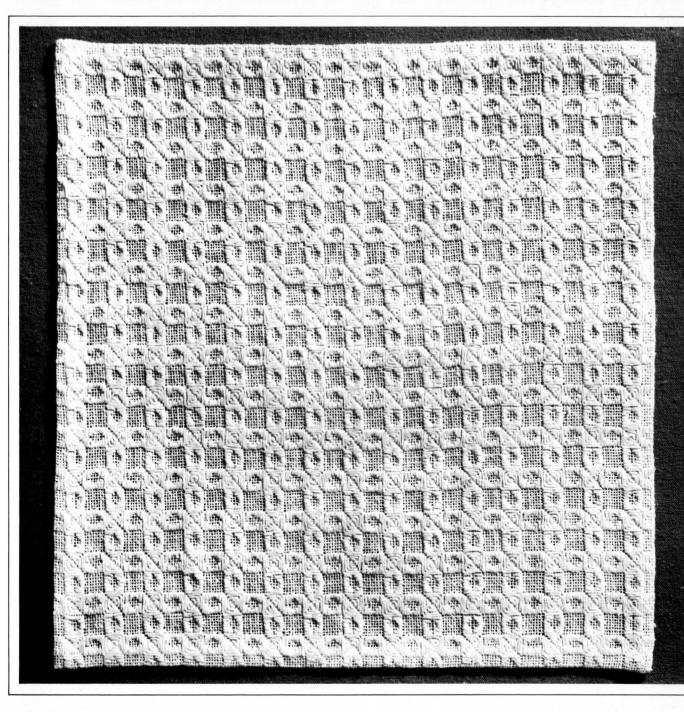

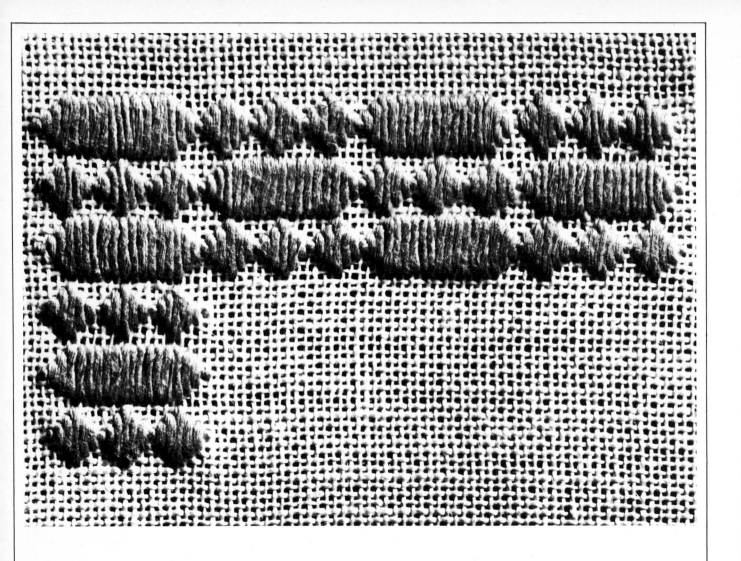

Mat for Breadbasket

Geometric Satin Stitch

Bleached D linen 55″ (140 cm) wide. Overall measurement $12\frac{1}{2}$″ $\times$ $12\frac{1}{2}$″ (32 $\times$ 32 cm). Finished work about $9\frac{3}{4}$″ $\times$ $9\frac{3}{4}$″ (24·5 $\times$ 24·5 cm). Linen thread quality E: red No. 41. Work with whole thickness. At upper left-hand corner of linen measure 2″ (5 cm) in from side edge and down from top edge. Start at this point. Hem: fold the material 7 threads from embroidery. Hem is 7 threads wide.

Placemat
Geometric Satin Stitch

Bleached D linen 11¾" (30 cm) wide. Overall measurement 11¾" × 19¾" (30 × 50 cm). Finished work 11¾" × 16½" (30 × 42 cm). Linen thread quality E. Work with half a strand. At upper left-hand corner of linen measure 2" (5 cm) in from side edge and start work 1 thread from selvedge. Finish with hemstitch over 2 threads right up to the embroidery. Hem is 6 threads wide.

Tea Cosy
Geometric Satin Stitch

Bleached D linen 55" (140 cm) wide. Overall measurement: 2 pieces 13¾" × 17" (35 × 43 cm), band 4¾" × 49¼" (12 × 125 cm). Finished work about 9¾" × 13¾" × 2" (25 × 33 × 5 cm). Linen thread quality E. Work with half a strand. At upper left-hand corner of linen measure 2" (5 cm) in from side edge and down from top edge. Start at this point. The seams are stitched 2 threads from the embroidery at the sides, and right up to the embroidery above and at the base. Band is 2" (5 cm) wide.

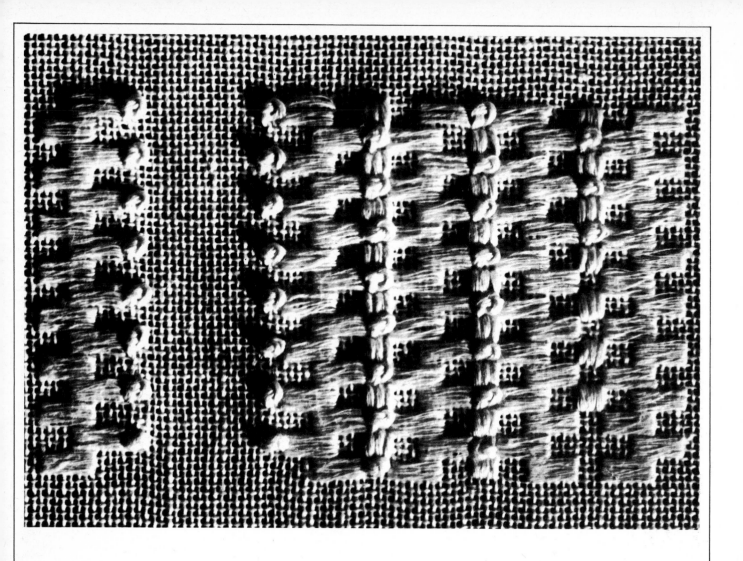

Tea Cosy
Geometric Satin Stitch and French Knots

Bleached D linen 55″ (140 cm) wide. Overall measurement $17\frac{3}{4}$″ $\times$ $25\frac{5}{8}$″ (45 $\times$ 65 cm) plus two pieces 6″ $\times$ $12\frac{5}{8}$″ (15 $\times$ 32 cm). Finished work $9\frac{5}{8}$″ $\times$ $13\frac{3}{4}$″ (24·5 $\times$ 35 cm). The side pieces are $9\frac{5}{8}$″ (24·5 cm) long, 2″ (5 cm) wide at the top, and $3\frac{3}{8}$″ (8·5 cm) wide at the bottom. Linen thread quality E. French knots are worked with 2 strands, satin stitch with half a strand. Find the centre of the material at the top and measure 2″ (5 cm) down. Start at this point. The embroidery is made in one piece, about $13\frac{3}{4}$″ $\times$ $21\frac{3}{4}$″ (35 $\times$ 55 cm). The seam is stitched close up to the embroidery.

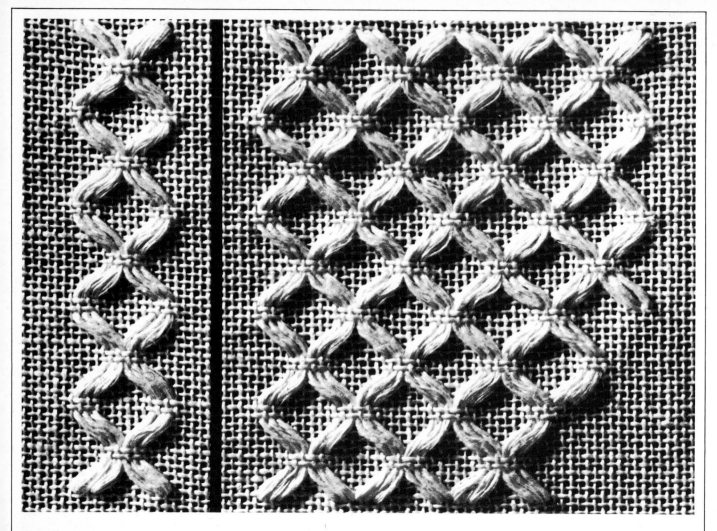

Tea Cosy
Darning Stitch

Bleached D linen 55″ (140 cm) wide. Overall measurement $17\frac{3}{4}″ \times 25\frac{5}{8}″$ (45 × 65 cm), plus 2 pieces 6″ × $12\frac{5}{8}″$ (15 × 32 cm). Finished work about $9\frac{5}{8}″ \times 13\frac{3}{8}″$ (24·5 × 34 cm). The side pieces are $9\frac{5}{8}″$ (24·5 cm) long, 2″ (5 cm) wide at the top, and $3\frac{3}{8}″$ (8·5 cm) wide at the bottom. Linen thread quality E. Work with whole thickness. Find the centre of the material at the top and measure 2″ (5 cm) down. Start the embroidery at this point. The embroidery is made in one piece – finished measurement about $13\frac{3}{8}″ \times 21\frac{3}{4}″$ (34 × 55 cm). The distance between the embroidery stripes is 22 threads. Make up with the seams 2 threads in from the embroidery at the sides, and close up to the embroidery at the base.

38

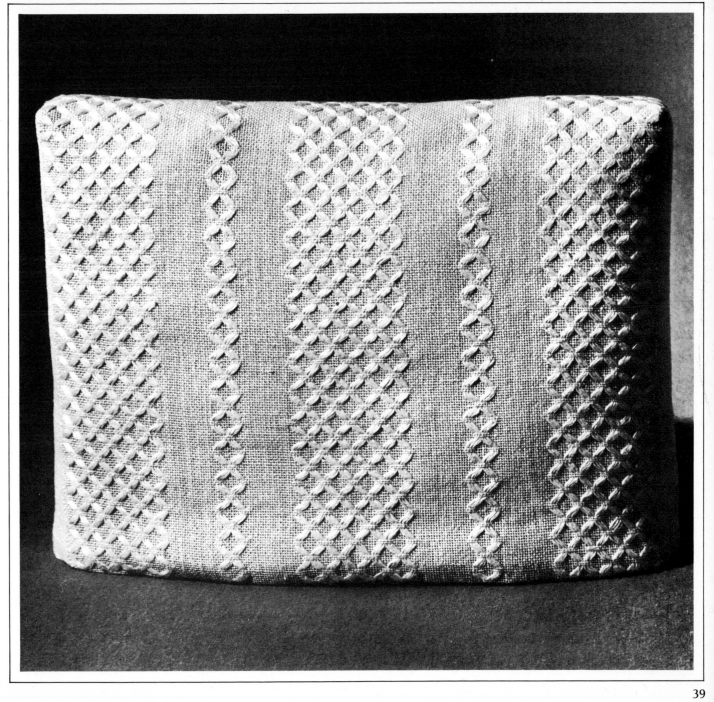

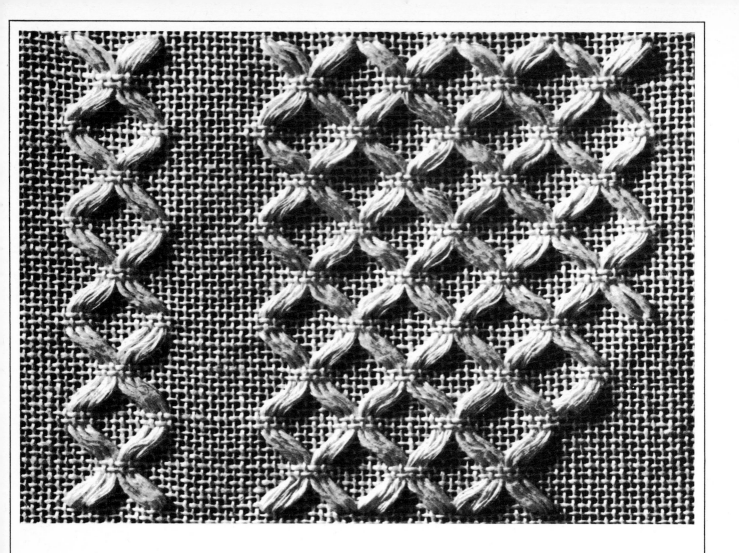

Tablecloth

Darning Stitch

Bleached D linen 55″ (140 cm) wide. Overall measurement 55″ × 78¾″ (140 × 200 cm). Finished work about 51″ × 72⅞″ (130 × 185 cm). Linen thread quality E. Work with whole thickness. Find the centre at the top of the material. Measure 3½″ (9 cm) in and start the embroidery at this point. Hem: fold the material 16 threads from embroidery. Finish with a hemstitch over 3 threads. Hem is 14 threads wide.

Tablecloth with Borders
Geometric Satin Stitch, Eye Stitch and French Knots

Bleached Hanne linen 63″ (160 cm) wide. Overall measurement 63″ × 95½″ (140 × 226 cm). Finished work about 55″ × 89¾″ (140 × 226 cm). Linen thread quality E and K. Eye stitch: work with 1 strand quality E. French knots and satin stitch: work with 2 strands quality K. There must be an even number of borders. The distance between the borders is 9⅝″ (24.5 cm). The width of each border is 1¾″ (4.5 cm). Mark centre of material lengthwise. Measure 4⅞″ (12.25 cm) from the centre to one of the sides, and 4″ (10 cm) in from one of the rough edges. Start a border at this point. When this border is finished, measure 9⅝″ (24.5 cm) along to the next. Hem: fold the material 1 thread from the embroidery lengthwise, and 3¾″ (9.5 cm) from the embroidery widthwise. Hem is 14 threads wide.

42

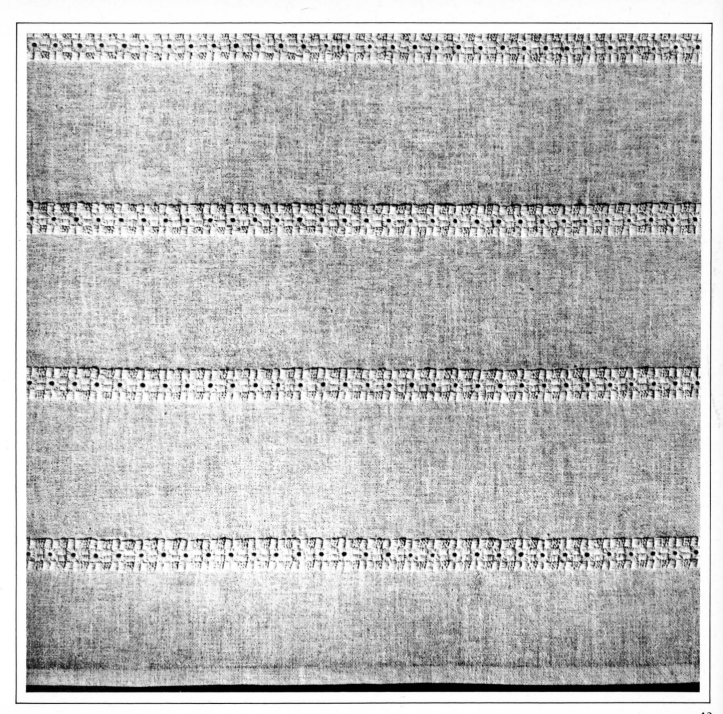

Tablecloth

Geometric Satin Stitch and Four-Sided Stitch

Bleached D linen 55″ (140 cm) wide. Overall measurement 55″ × 80¾″ (140 × 205 cm). Finished work about 51″ × 74¾″ (130 × 190 cm). Linen thread quality E. Work with whole thickness. Find the centre at the top of the material. Measure 4″ (10 cm) in and start to work at this point. The four-sided stitches are worked before the threads are drawn out. Work four-sided stitch round the cloth. Hem: fold the material 16 threads from the four-sided stitch. Hem is 16 threads wide.

44

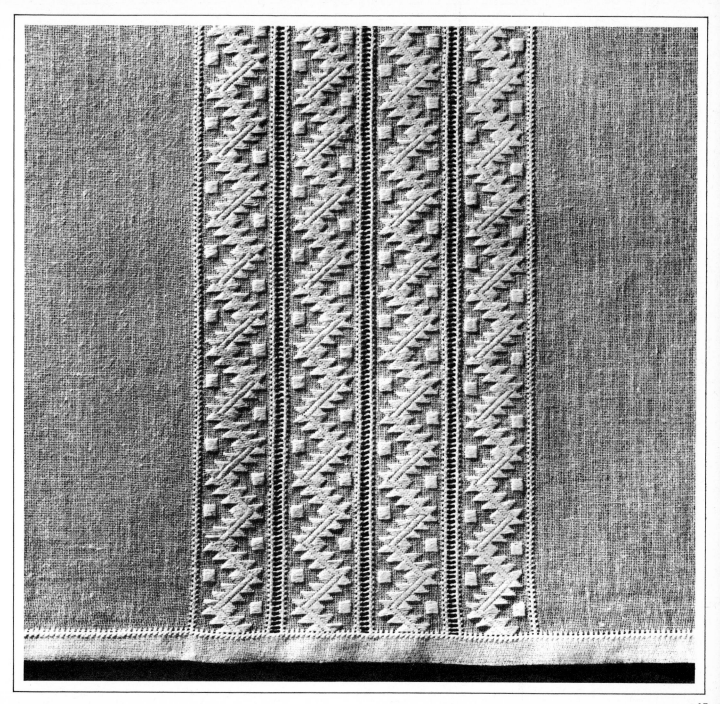

45

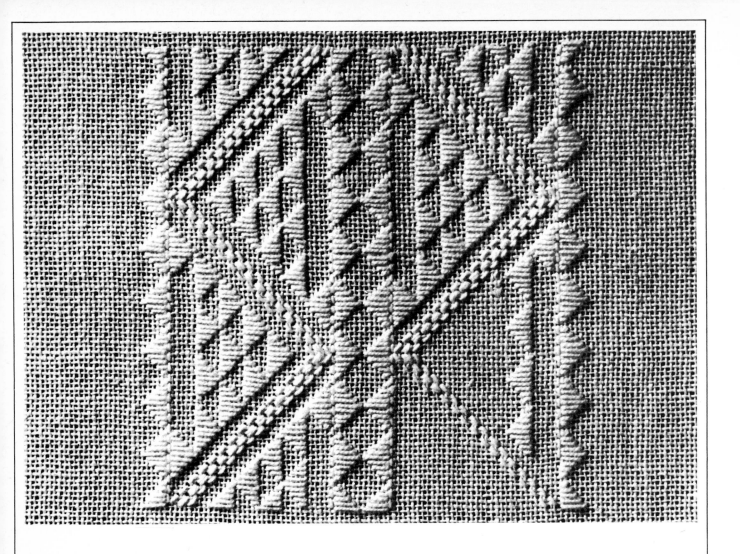

Tablecloth for a Narrow Table
Geometric Satin Stitch and Reversed Faggot Stitch

Bleached D linen 55″ (140 cm) wide. Overall measurement $41\frac{3}{8}″ \times 82\frac{3}{4}″$ (105×210 cm). Finished work about $31\frac{1}{2}″ \times 77\frac{1}{4}″$ (80×196 cm). Cotton thread. Work with 1 strand. Mark the centre at the top of the material. Measure 4″ (10 cm) in and begin the middle border at this point. Satin stitch triangles are worked all the way round. The distance from the middle border to the triangles is 8 threads. Hem: fold the material 1 thread from the triangles all the way round. Finish with a hemstitch over 2 threads. Hem is 13 threads wide.

Tablecloth with Borders

Geometric Satin Stitch

Bleached D linen 55″ (140 cm) wide. Overall measurement 55″ × 80¾″ (140 × 205 cm). Finished work about 51″ × 74¾″ (130 × 190 cm). Linen thread quality E. Work with whole thickness. Mark the centre at the top of the material. Measure 4″ (10 cm) in and start to work at this point. Fold the material 20 threads from the embroidery. Finish with a hemstitch over 3 threads. Hem is 18 threads wide.

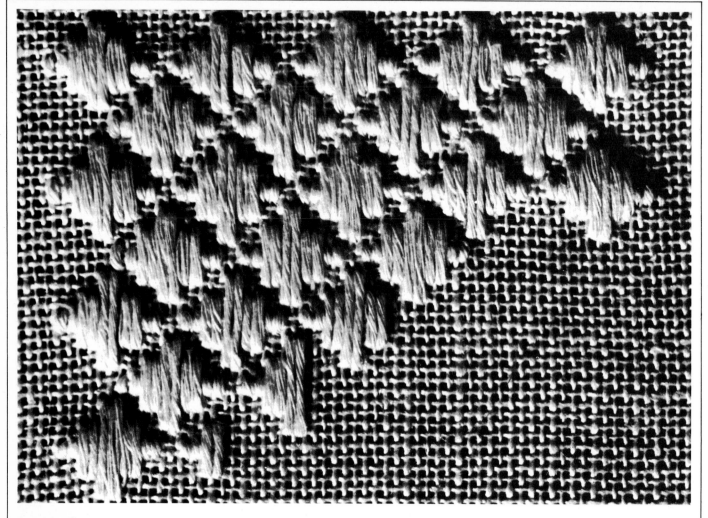

Tablecloth with Borders

Geometric Satin Stitch

Bleached D linen 55″ (140 cm) wide. Overall measurement 55″ × 95½″ (140 × 240 cm). Finished work about 50½″ × 89¾″ (128 × 226 cm). Linen thread quality E. Work with whole thickness. There must be an even number of borders. The distance between borders is 9″ (23 cm). Each border is 2⅜″ (6 cm) wide. Mark centre of material lengthwise. Measure 4″ (10 cm) in from one of the rough edges, and 4½″ (11·5 cm) from the centre to one of the sides. Start a border at this point. When this border is finished measure 9″ (23 cm) along to the next. Hem: fold the material lengthwise 20 threads from the embroidery, and 3⅜″ (8·5 cm) from the embroidery widthwise. Hem is 17 threads wide. Finish with hemstitch over 3 threads.

Tablecloth with counted thread embroidery borders worked with yellow or white linen thread. The space between the borders must be sufficient to allow room for a plate, as on a placemat. Calculate the distance between the pairs of borders according to the length of the table.

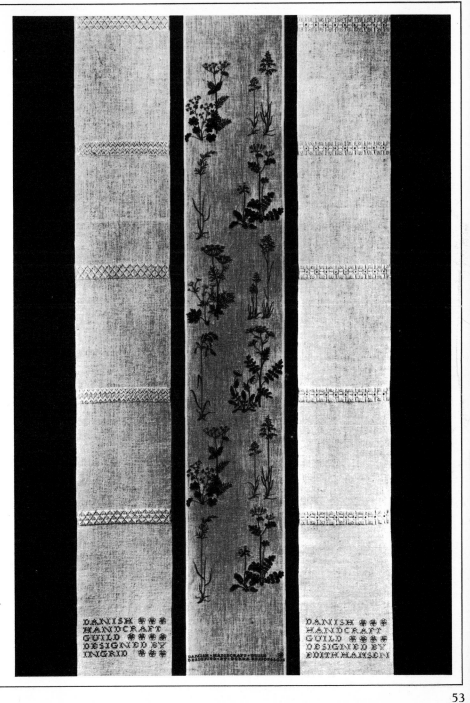

Exhibits from 'A Century of Danish Design', held in 1968 at the Victoria and Albert Museum, London, showing one of the many possibilities for using borders. In the centre are Gerda Bengtsson's grasses and wild flowers in greens and yellows.

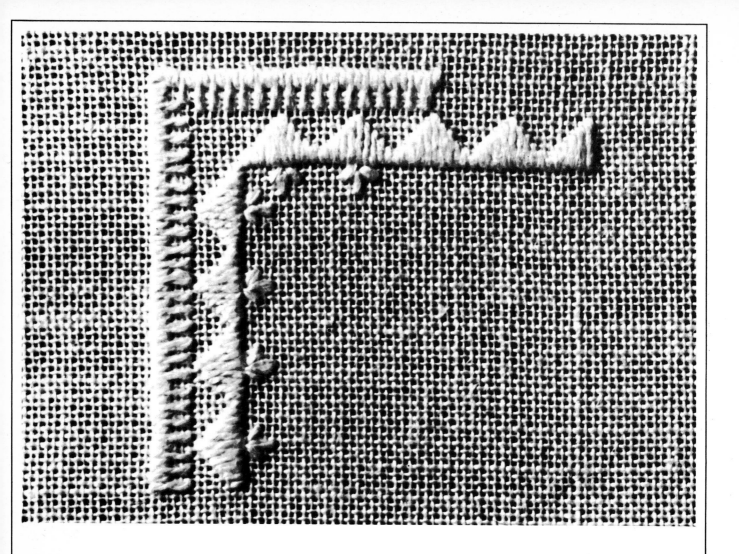

Friendship Cloth

Geometric Satin Stitch

Bleached D linen 55″ (140 cm) wide. Overall measurement $15\frac{3}{8}″ \times 15\frac{3}{8}″$ (29 × 29 cm) for each little square. Linen thread quality K. Work with 1 strand. At upper left-hand corner of linen measure 2″ (5 cm) in from side edge and down from top edge. Start at this point. Hem: fold the material right up to the embroidery. Hem is 6 threads wide. The squares are joined by overcasting.

See also the illustration on page 70.

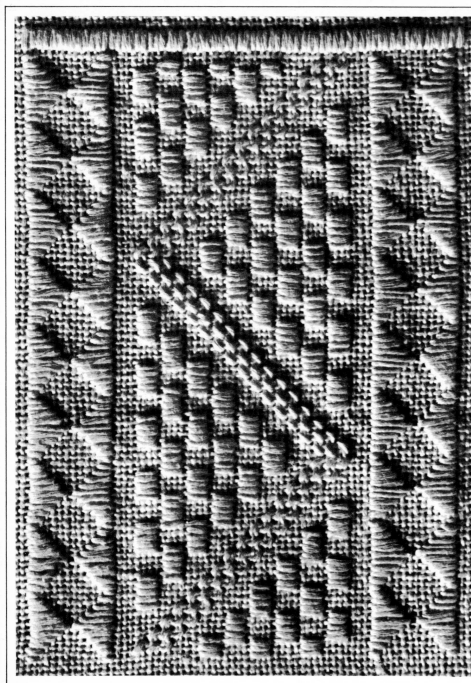

Table Runner

Geometric Satin Stitch

Bleached Hanne linen 63″ (160 cm) wide. Overall measurement $12\frac{5}{8}″ \times 61\frac{3}{4}″$ (32 × 157 cm). Finished work about $8\frac{3}{4}″ \times 57\frac{3}{4}″$ (22 × 147 cm). Linen thread quality E. Work with whole thickness. At upper left-hand corner of linen measure 2″ (5 cm) in from side edge and down from top edge. Start at this point. Hem: fold the material 1 thread from embroidery all the way round. Hem: 14 threads wide lengthwise, 7 threads width-wise.

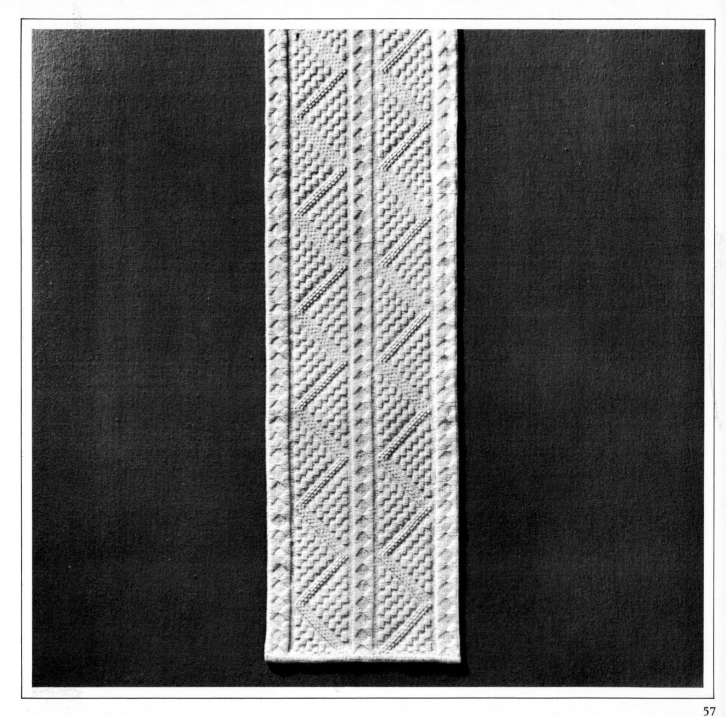

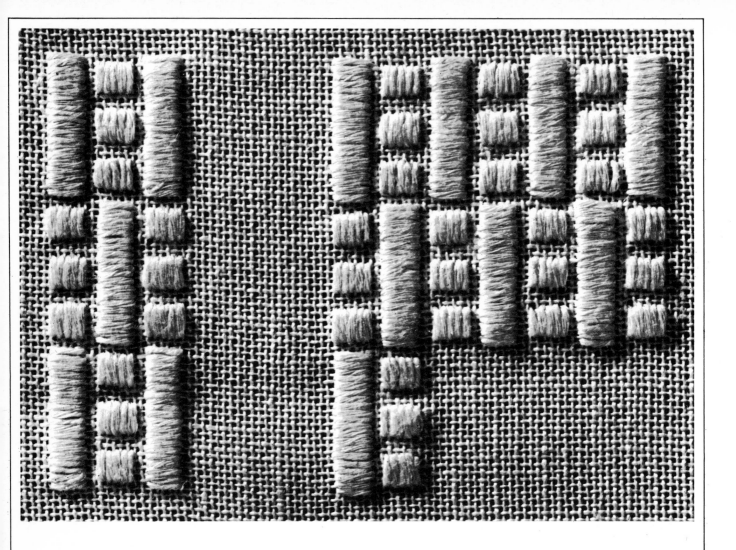

Table Runner
Geometric Satin Stitch
Bleached D linen $7\frac{1}{8}''$ (18 cm) wide. Overall measurement $7\frac{1}{8}'' \times 72\frac{3}{4}''$ (18 × 185 cm). Finished work about $7\frac{1}{8}'' \times 60\frac{5}{8}''$ (18 × 154 cm). Linen thread quality E. Work with whole thickness. Find the exact centre at top of linen, measure $6''$ (15 cm) down and start the embroidery at this point. Knot the fringe at the ends of the runner 5 threads away from embroidery, with 8 threads in each bunch.

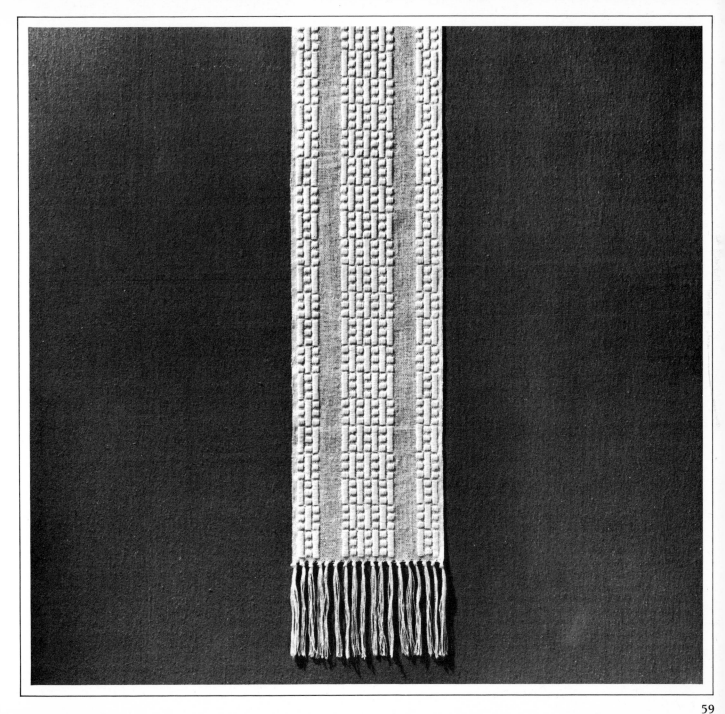

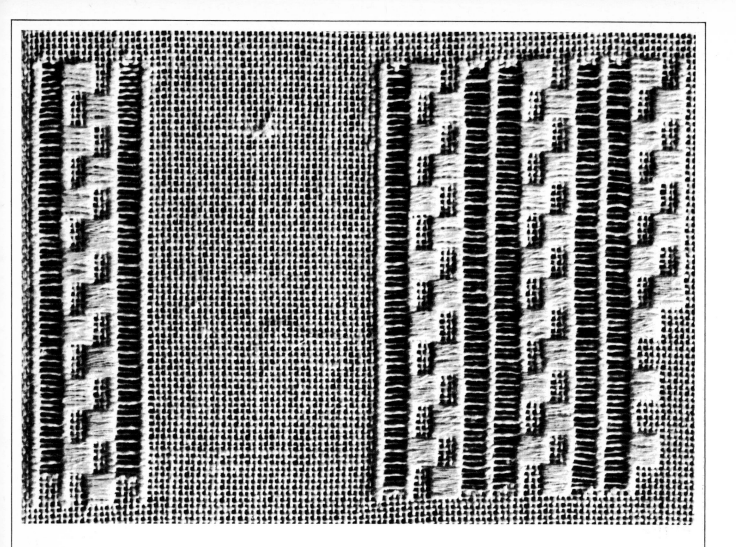

Table Runner
Geometric Satin Stitch and Hemstitch

Bleached D linen 55″ (140 cm) wide. Overall measurement $20\frac{3}{4}″ \times 78\frac{3}{4}″$ (53 × 200 cm). Finished work about $17\frac{1}{2}″ \times 63″$ (45 × 160 cm) plus fringe $6\frac{3}{4}″$ (17 cm). Linen thread quality E. Work with whole thickness. Measure 7″ (18 cm) down from the top of the material, find the middle and start at this point. The threads are drawn out when the embroidery has been finished. Fold the material at the sides 6 threads from the embroidery. Hem is 6 threads wide. Finish runner with a fringe at ends by unravelling the material until 3 threads away from embroidery. Tie the knots with 5 threads in each bunch.

Hat

Darning Stitch and Beads

Bleached Hanne linen 63″ (160 cm) wide. White beads. Overall measurement $27\frac{1}{2}″ \times 7\frac{1}{8}″$ (70 × 18 cm) plus $9\frac{3}{4}″ \times 9\frac{3}{4}″$ (25 × 25 cm). Finished work about $3\frac{1}{8}″$ (8 cm) in height. Circumference of crown 22″ (56 cm). Linen thread quality E. Work with 2 strands. At the upper left-hand corner of the long piece of linen, measure 2″ (5 cm) in from side edge and down from top edge. Start to work at this point. Embroider a piece about $23\frac{3}{4}″$ (60 cm) long. For the crown, draw a circle 8″ (20 cm) in diameter. Cover it with darning stitches to fit the shape of the hat, before the beads are worked on.

Bag

Darning Stitch and Beads

Bleached Hanne linen 63″ (160 cm) wide. White beads. Overall measurement $23\frac{5}{8}″ \times 14\frac{1}{4}″$ (60 × 36 cm) plus $9\frac{3}{4}″ \times 9\frac{3}{4}″$ (25 × 25 cm). Finished work 7″ (18 cm) in height, bottom $6\frac{1}{8}″$ (15·5 cm) wide. Linen thread quality E. Work with 2 strands. At upper left-hand corner of linen measure 2″ (5 cm) in from side edge and down from top edge. Start at this point and embroider a piece measuring 7″ × $19\frac{3}{4}″$ (18 × 50 cm). The flap that fastens the bag is worked at one end of the strip, above the main area of the embroidery. Matching the pattern, work evenly up to a point from a base 6″ (15 cm) in width. The height from the base of the flap to its point is about 4″ (10 cm). Materials and instructions for making up may be obtained from the Danish Handcraft Guild. (See page 76).

Mirror
Geometric Satin Stitch and French Knots

Bleached Hanne linen 63″ (160 cm) wide. Overall measurement $18\frac{1}{2}″ \times 20\frac{3}{4}″$ (47 × 53 cm). Finished work $14\frac{1}{4}″ \times 17″$ (36·5 × 43 cm). Linen thread quality K and S.K is worked with 1 strand for satin stitch, 2 strands for French knots. S No. 585 is worked with 3 strands for satin stitch, 4 strands for French knots. At upper left-hand corner of linen measure 2″ (5 cm) from side edge and down from top edge. Start at this point. See page 68 for instructions on making up.

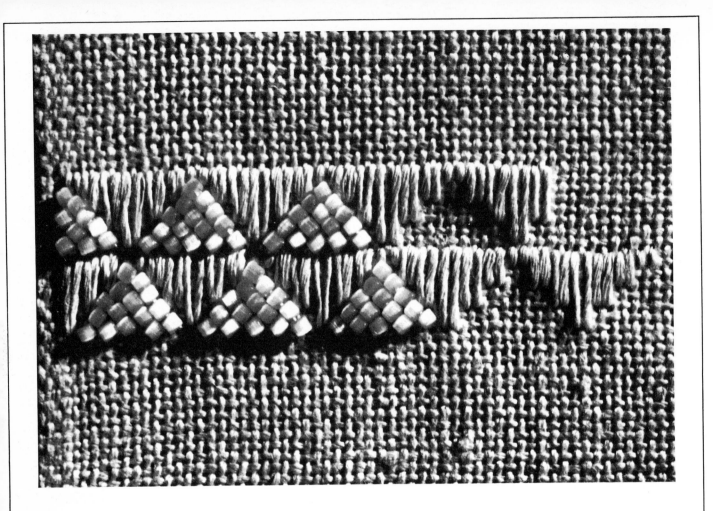

Bag

Geometric Satin Stitch

Unbleached Hanne linen 63″ (160 cm) wide. White beads. Overall measurement 13″ × 18½″ (33 × 47 cm) plus 2 gusset pieces for the sides. Finished work about 6¾″ × 8⅞″ (17 × 22·5 cm). Linen thread quality E. Geometric satin stitch is worked with whole thickness. Beads are stitched on with 2 strands of stranded cotton At upper left-hand corner of linen measure 2″ (5 cm) in from side edge and down from top edge. Start at this point. The bag is made in one piece. Twelve stripes constitute half of the pattern; the other 12 stripes are worked in reverse. Materials and instructions for making up may be obtained from the Danish Handcraft Guild. (See page 76).

Mounting the Mirrors

When the embroidery is finished press it well on the wrong side over a damp cloth; then measure the length and width of the embroidery very precisely.

Get a glazier to cut a mirror to fit this measurement. Cut a piece of cardboard about $\frac{1}{20}''$ (1 mm) thick to fit the back of the mirror. Glue it on firmly. Fasten a strip of thick gummed paper or carpet binding round the edge of the mirror and the cardboard to prevent the sharp edges of the mirror from fraying the embroidery. Now take the embroidery and cut round it, leaving a margin of 4″ (10 cm) for folding. Cut in the middle, as shown in the photograph, $1\frac{1}{4}$″ (3 cm) from the embroidery. Corners should be cut to 1 thread away from the embroidery. Fray corners carefully and fold the fringes over to the wrong side, where they must be carefully tacked down. The straight sides should also be folded over and tacked down.

Buy about 2 yds (2 m) of tape 2″ (5 cm) wide. Cut 4 pieces the same length as the sides of the embroidery, including the folds. Fasten these pieces on to the wrong side, $\frac{3}{8}$″ (1 cm) inside the inner edge of the embroidery. They should be stitched on firmly here to keep the edges tight. It is only necessary to stitch them on the inside. Now place the embroidery over the mirror. Fasten it all round with pins so that the edge of the embroidery lies right next to the edge of the mirror. Pins can be fixed into the cardboard. When this has been done, turn the mirror face down. Take the loose hanging tapes and fold them as tightly as possible round on to the wrong side. Fasten them first with pins. Then glue them on, unpinning one corner at a time. Use pins again to support the embroidery until the glue is quite dry. Then turn the outer edge of the embroidery over to the back, and glue this firmly in the same way, doing one side at a time and using pins for tacking. Cut away a little of the superfluous material from the corners.

For covering the back of the mirror use a piece of strong linen. In the centre of the back, and about $1\frac{1}{2}$″ (3 cm) from the top, stitch on a small curtain ring very firmly. Tack or pin on the backing starting with the place where the ring has been positioned, to make sure it is dead centre. Stitch the backing on all the way round.

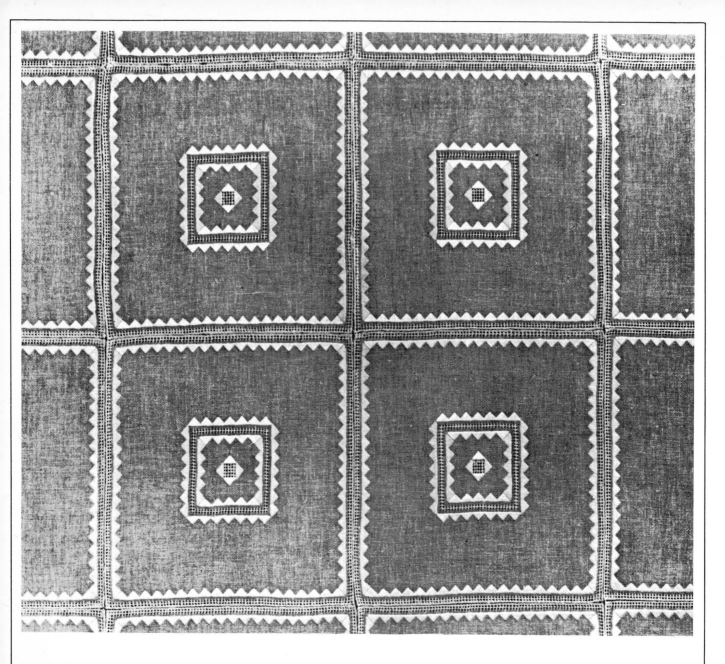

Detail of a friendship tablecloth by Gertie Wandel, composed of 60 embroidered squares. Years ago these tablecloths used to be presented by a large circle of friends as a joint gift at family celebrations.

Hemstitch

This may be worked with or without pulling out threads, and over a varying number of threads. Hemstitch is worked from the reverse side. (a) The needle is passed under a group of threads. (b) Then 1 thread is stitched down into the hem.

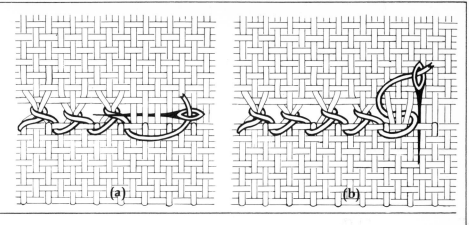

Long-Armed Cross-Stitch

This stitch is worked in horizontal rows from left to right; (a) and (b) show the slightly irregular beginning. Thereafter work alternately as shown in drawings (c) and (d).

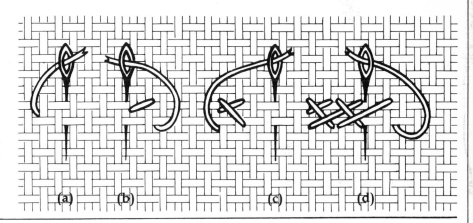

Bead Embroidery

(a) Rows from left to right: stitch beads on with half a cross-stitch. (b) Rows from right to left: stitch beads on with petit point stitch on the straight. In bead embroidery with triangles, the beads will appear to greater advantage if a thread is drawn through the diagonal rows of beads after the beads have been stitched on.

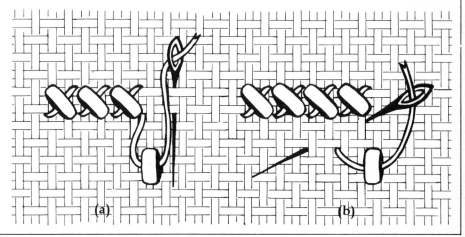

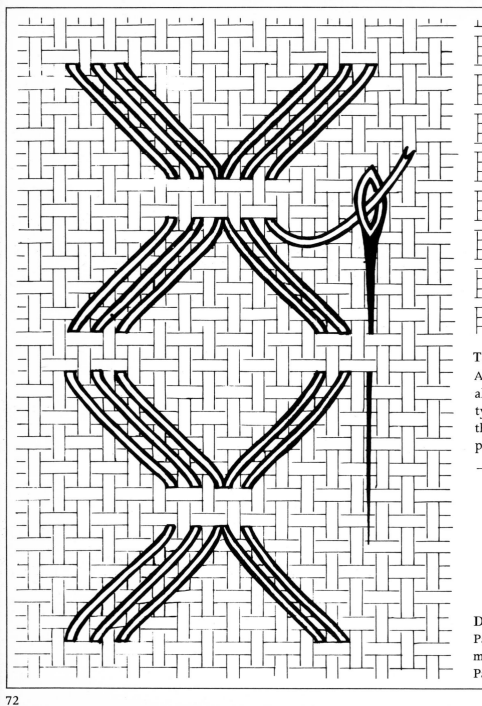

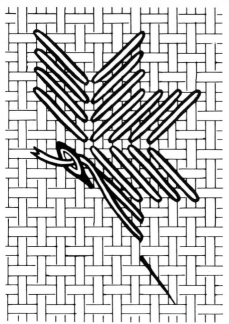

The Star

All the stitches must be taken diagonally over 3 crossings of threads. In this type of counted thread embroidery the best result is obtained by not pulling the thread too tight.

Darning Stitch

Pass needle under 2 threads of the material. Count 4 threads diagonally. Pass again under 2 threads of material.

Backstitch

Work each stitch back over 2 threads.
Pass needle forward under 4 threads.

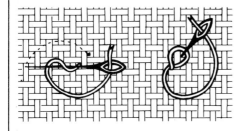

French Knots

Pull up the needle on the right side of the material. Hold the thread parallel to material between left thumb and forefinger. Then pass the needle under and over the thread. Turn the needle as indicated by the arrow on the drawing, and draw it down 1 thread further on. Do not release thread (held in left hand) until the knot has been drawn tight.

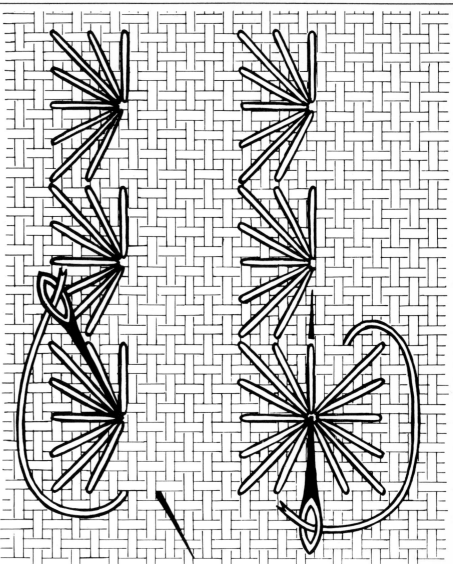

Eye Stitch

True eye stitch consists of 16 stitches, but the name is still used when more or fewer are used. The stitches are done over a square of threads, all starting from the edges and meeting in the centre of the square. A row of eyelet stitches is worked in 2 journeys, making the embroidery look the same on both the right and wrong sides.

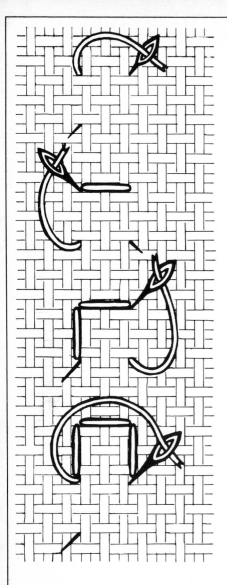

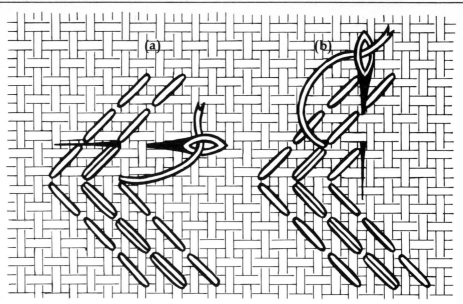

Reversed Faggot Stitch

Pass needle under 2 threads, alternately horizontally (a) and vertically (b). Reversed faggot stitch is stitched in 2 journeys whereby all centre stitches are doubled. All stitches on the right side are diagonal.

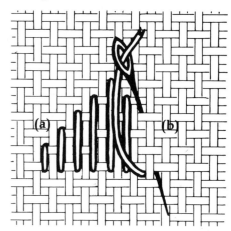

Four-Sided Stitch or Square Stitch

Pass the needle slantwise under 3 threads. All stitches on the right side are either vertical or horizontal. All stitches on the reverse are diagonal.

Geometric Satin Stitch

Pass the needle through 4 threads up and 1 along the material, making the stitches on the right side vertical. Triangles are made by working each stitch (a) 1 thread higher, or (b) 1 thread lower.

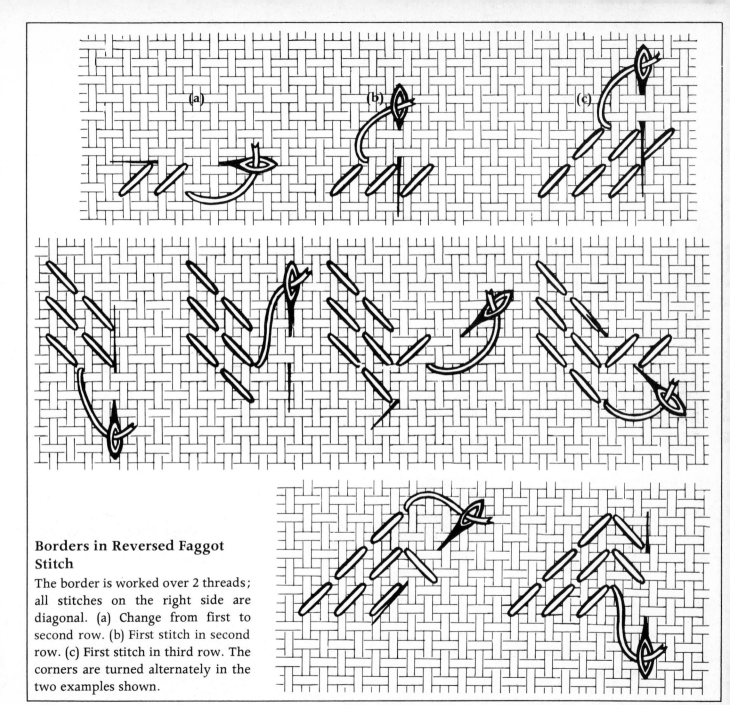

Borders in Reversed Faggot Stitch

The border is worked over 2 threads; all stitches on the right side are diagonal. (a) Change from first to second row. (b) First stitch in second row. (c) First stitch in third row. The corners are turned alternately in the two examples shown.

Materials

For the embroidery in this book use bleached and unbleached Hanne linen, 13 threads to the inch (5 threads to the cm). It comes in widths of 63″ (160 cm) and 13″ (33 cm).

Bleached and unbleached D linen, 18 threads to the inch (7 threads to the cm). This comes in widths of 55″ (140 cm), $11\frac{3}{4}$″ (30 cm) and 7″ (18 cm); the latter is handwoven bleached.

Various qualities of linen thread (E, K, S and Y) are used for the embroidery. Beads.

Use a No. 20 tapestry needle (without point) on Hanne linen; and a No. 22 on D linen.

Materials and thread obtainable from the Danish Handcraft Guild, Vimmelskaftet 38, 1161 Copenhagen K, Denmark. Danish linens are available from Mace & Nairn, 89 Crane Street, Salisbury, Wilts., England and at the USA Artisan's Guild, 10B Street, Burlington, Massachusetts, USA.

Laundering

Linen should be washed in soap flakes. It must never be boiled or washed in detergents as this dries the flax fibres and reduces the durability of the material. It is not advisable to wring the washed article; it is better to press out the moisture carefully and put the article to dry between two white cloths.

Ironing

Place embroidery face down on a soft pad. Cover with a well-wrung damp cloth, and iron until the cloth is dry. Then iron directly on the reverse side of the embroidery until this too is quite dry. Take care that the grain of the linen lies straight while it is being ironed.

Stretching

Small items will appear to much greater advantage if they are stretched rather than ironed, as both linen and embroidery will stand out in bolder relief. For stretching use a wooden board covered with white paper, and several stainless steel pins or drawing pins. The embroidery is placed face down on the board and stretched at right angles. Place the pins very close together. Cover the embroidery with a well-wrung damp towel or other cloth. The whole thing must be absolutely dry before the pins are removed – this takes about 24 hours.